Bond

UP TO *SPEED*
Verbal
Reasoning
Tests and Papers

8–9 years

Frances Down

Nelson Thornes

Published in 2013 by:
Nelson Thornes Ltd
Delta Place
27 Bath Road
CHELTENHAM
GL53 7TH
United Kingdom

13 14 15 16 17 / 10 9 8 7 6 5 4 3 2 1

A catalogue record for this book is available from the British Library

ISBN 978 1 4085 1882 3

Page make-up by OKS Prepress, India

Printed in China by 1010 Printing International Ltd

Introduction

What is Bond?

The Bond *Up to Speed* series is a new addition to the Bond range of assessment papers, the number one series for the 11+, selective exams and general practice. Bond *Up to Speed* is carefully designed to support children who need less challenging activities than those in the regular age-appropriate Bond papers, in order to build up and improve their techniques and confidence.

How does this book work?

The book contains two distinct sets of papers, along with full answers and a Progress Chart.

- Focus tests, accompanied by advice and directions, are focused on particular (and age-appropriate) verbal reasoning question types encountered in the 11+ and other exams. The questions are deliberately set at a less challenging level than the standard *Assessment Papers*. Each Focus test is designed to help a child 'catch' their level in a particular question type, and then gently raise it through the course of the test and the subsequent Mixed papers.

- Mixed papers are longer tests containing a full range of verbal reasoning question types. These are designed to provide rigorous practice with less challenging questions, perhaps against the clock, in order to help children acquire and develop the necessary skills and techniques for 11+ success.

Full answers are provided for both types of test in the middle of the book.

How much time should the tests take?

The tests are for practice and to reinforce learning, and you may wish to test exam techniques and working to a set time limit. Using the Mixed papers, we would recommend that your child spends 40 minutes answering the 45 questions in each paper.

You can reduce the suggested time by 5 minutes to practise working at speed.

Using the Progress Chart

The Progress Chart can be used to track Focus test and Mixed paper results over time to monitor how well your child is doing and identify any repeated problems in tackling the different question types.

A B C D E F G H I J K L M N O P Q R S T U V W X Y Z

If these words are placed in alphabetical order, underline the word that comes first.

> The alphabet has been written out to help you. Scan the line quickly and check your choice carefully.

1	walk	fear	make	ally	sure
2	poor	hood	room	good	book
3	tiny	dear	lord	vine	pond
4	beak	door	axle	card	evil
5	ugly	crab	mild	fish	gone

5

In each line, underline the word that has its letters in alphabetical order.

6	slap	tray	dewy	much
7	loot	nude	jump	yell
8	made	belt	mile	bung
9	quit	envy	jeer	quay
10	hunt	hand	help	hill

5

Imagine the first two letters of the alphabet are removed. Answer these questions.

> Cover the first two letters in the alphabet above and then count carefully.

11 Which would be the third letter of those left? Circle the correct letter.

B   E   H   C

12 How many letters would there be in this alphabet? Circle the correct number.

24   26   23   25

Imagine the last two letters of the alphabet are removed. Answer these questions.

> This time cover the last two letters in the alphabet.

13 Which would be the last letter of those left? Circle the correct letter.

V   U   X   W

14 Which is the middle letter of the new alphabet?

H   N   O   L

4

Answer these alphabet questions.

15 Which month of the year begins with the fifteenth letter? _____

16 Which month of the year begins with the
nineteenth letter?   _____

17 Which day of the week has nine letters?   _____

18 If the days of the week are put in alphabetical order,
which comes last?   _____

19 If the seasons are put in alphabetical order,
which comes last?   _____

5

If the letters in the following words are arranged in alphabetical order, which letter comes last?

> Write the letters of the word in alphabetical order, then select the last one.

20 MARCH ____   **21** SOUTH ____   **22** DEATH ____

23 BANKS ____   **24** ZEBRA ____

5

Underline the word in each line that uses only the first six letters of the alphabet.

25 tab   hut   bed   van

26 cab   cat   car   can

27 zoo   jut   mix   bad

> Write the first
> six letters of the
> alphabet and then
> check carefully.

3

Underline the word in each line that uses three vowels.

> Write down the vowels and then count how many there are in each word.
> Some vowels may be repeated. These should still be counted.

28 garden   hurtle   brandy   melons   beetle

29 kettle   verges   alcove   throat   supple

30 choice   pearls   broken   ghosts   milked

3

Focus test 2 Similars and opposites

Always read this type of question carefully, as most will have similar <u>and</u> opposite options.

Underline the two words, one from each group, that are the most similar in meaning.

Example (race, shop, <u>start</u>) (finish, <u>begin</u>, end)

Compare the first word in the left brackets with each word in the right brackets. Repeat with the other two words in the left brackets until you find a pair of similar words.

1 (shiny, dull, fun)   (mild, damp, bright)

2 (dark, rob, call)   (pull, steal, give)

3 (shout, buy, kiss)   (try, mix, scream)

4 (howl, mend, jump)   (leap, quick, bring)

5 (bite, quick, mask)   (steady, swift, choose)   **5**

Underline the two words, one from each group, that are the most opposite in meaning.

Example (dawn, <u>early</u>, wake) (<u>late</u>, stop, sunrise)

6 (sleep, awake, fast)   (brisk, slow, race)

7 (kind, mind, bind)   (mental, sort, cruel)   Take care. Opposites this time.

8 (up, under, through)   (down, put, calm)

9 (fair, fire, full)   (empty, complete, whole)

10 (trip, clean, buy)   (spotless, sell, stumble)   **5**

Underline the pair of words that are the most similar in meaning.

Example come, go   <u>roams, wanders</u>   fear, fare

11 hard, soft   male, female   easy, simple   Look for the <u>most</u> similar pair of words.

12 heavy, light   neat, tidy   back, front

13 hurry, rush   help, heal   cry, laugh

14 bring, buy   fix, mix   try, attempt

15 correct, wrong   crazy, mad   four, for   **5**

Underline the pair of words that are the most opposite in meaning.

Example   cup, mug   coffee, milk   <u>hot, cold</u>

16   tall, short   stout, fat   clever, intelligent

17   quick, quite   lithe, soothe   fair, dark

18   top, high   left, right   aim, strive

19   yes, no   big, huge   misty, foggy

20   if, where   in, out   to, too

> Take care.
> Opposites
> this time.

5

Underline the one word in the brackets that is the most similar in meaning to the word in capitals.

Example   UNHAPPY   (unkind   death   laughter   <u>sad</u>   friendly)

> Look at each word in the brackets in turn. Pick the <u>most</u> similar.

21   STOP   (go   halt   burst   look   start)

22   DIFFERENT   (alike   similar   unlike   dislike   same)

23   RAPID   (pace   hard   nice   fast   grand)

24   START   (begin   end   note   climb   press)

25   LARGE   (tiny   huge   small   need   keep)

5

Underline the one word in the brackets that is the most opposite in meaning to the word in capitals.

Example   WIDE   (broad   vague   long   <u>narrow</u>   motorway)

> Pick the <u>most</u> opposite.

26   FAT   (skin   wide   fresh   hunger   thin)

27   ROUGH   (jagged   bumpy   smooth   fierce   brisk)

28   BLACK   (night   dark   day   evil   white)

29   DIRTY   (grubby   clean   dusty   lift   drop)

30   COVERED   (lid   bare   blanket   hidden   under)

5

Focus test 3 — Sorting words

Look at these groups of words.

A	B	C
Fruit	Furniture	Days of the week

Choose the correct group for each of the words below. Write in the letter.

1 table   ____   apple   ____

2 Saturday   ____   bed   ____

3 banana   ____   Monday   ____

4 peach   ____   chair   ____

5 Friday   ____   orange   ____

5

Underline the two words that are the odd ones out in the following group of words.

Example black   king   purple   green   house

Find the link between three of the words. In the example, it is colours.

6 table   knife   fork   spoon   chair

7 orange   pasta   noodles   apple   grapes

8 dog   pet   cat   animal   hamster

9 car   lorry   van   road   tree

10 twenty   mole   sixteen   eight   beetle

5

Underline the two words in each sentence that need to change places for the sentence to make sense.

Example She went to letter the write.

Read the sentence carefully and identify where it does not make sense.

11 The road crossed the boy carefully.

12 Do enjoy you reading about famous people?

13 Look at all the trees falling off the leaves!

14 A black cat crept along the top of the wall garden.

15 Please close in and come the door quietly.

5

Fill in the crosswords so that all the given words are included. You have been given one letter as a clue in each crossword.

16

■	■		
M			

MOLE
GRIP
GLUM
POLE

17

	■		■
			M
	■	■	

CALM
BACK
BENT
NILL

18

			F
	■	■	

LIAR
ROOF
RAIL
FAIR

19

■		■	
■	C	■	

QUIT
SUCH
STUN
THAN

20

	■	■	
S	■	■	

TENT
POOL
LEFT
PAST

> Use the given letter to place the first word.

5

Rearrange the muddled words in capital letters so that each sentence makes sense.

Example There are sixty SNODCES <u>seconds</u> in a UTMINE <u>minute</u>.

> Use the sense of the sentence to help you. Be careful with spelling.

21 My cat has FTOS _____ fur and a long LITA _____.

22 He put a slice of EMONL _____ in his KDRNI _____.

23 Seven take away RFUO _____ equals ERETH _____.

24 Our SEUOH _____ has a newly painted front OROD _____.

25 She dived into the LOPO _____ and WAMS _____ lengths.

5

Underline the two words in each line that are made from the same letters.

Example	TAP	PET	<u>TEA</u>	POT	<u>EAT</u>
26	TIME	MITE	MATE	NOUN	NAIL
27	MARE	MANE	NAIL	NAME	RAIN
28	COOK	COOL	LOOP	LOOK	POOL
29	LAIR	LAID	DIAL	HAIL	DARE
30	AGED	RAGE	PEAR	GEAR	GAPE

5

Now go to the Progress Chart to record your score! Total **30**

Rearrange the muddled letters in capitals to make a proper word. The answer will complete the sentence sensibly.

Example   A BEZAR is an animal with stripes.   ZEBRA

> Look at the sense of the sentence and then rearrange the letters.

1   A HRCIA is a seat with four legs.   _____

2   A REDPIS has eight legs.   _____

3   LLOYEW is a primary colour.   _____

4   A VRDEI is an area outside a house for cars.   _____

5   There are twenty-six TTELRSE in the alphabet.   _____

6   A PRADOEL is a big cat with a spotted coat.   _____   **6**

Which one letter can be added to the front of all of these words to make new words?

Example   Care   Cat   Crate   Call   C

> Experiment with putting various letters in front of each of the words until you find the correct one.

7   __listen   __rumble   __laze   __ear   ____

8   __ramp   __lever   __lump   __one   ____

9   __and   __arm   __ill   __ant   ____

10   __right   __lake   __lame   __eel   ____

11   __ink   __each   __earl   __ray   ____

12   __earth   __ill   __eating   __itch   ____   **6**

Find the letter that will end the first word and start the second word.

Example drow (<u>n</u>) ought

> Look at the word on the left and find various letters that could finish that word. Then see which one will also start the word on the right.

13 lorr (__) oung

14 gues (__) orry

15 flowe (__) aspberry

16 snai (__) abel

17 snif (__) luffy

18 dancin (__) lass

6

Add one letter to the word in capital letters to make a new word. The meaning of the new word is given in the clue.

Example PLAN   simple   <u>PLAIN</u>

> Look at the meaning and find a word that uses the letters given on the left.

19 ART   a section of   _____

20 FIST   at the beginning   _____

21 PIKE   pointed piece of metal   _____

22 FLEE   a group of ships   _____

23 STAR   begin   _____

24 BEAK   stop for a rest   _____

6

Remove one letter from the word in capital letters to leave a new word. The meaning of the new word is given in the clue.

Example AUNT   an insect   <u>ANT</u>

25 QUITE   stop   _____

26 CLIMB   body part   _____

27 NEVER   always   _____

28 GRAZE   look at   _____

29 SPELL   exchange for money   _____

30 BROOK   reading material   _____

6

Now go to the Progress Chart to record your score!   Total   30

11

Focus test 5 Selecting words

Complete the following sentences by selecting the most sensible word from each group of words given in the brackets. Underline the words selected.

Example The (<u>children</u>, boxes, foxes) carried the (houses, <u>books</u>, steps) home from the (greengrocer, <u>library</u>, factory).

> Work through each sentence, bracket by bracket, choosing the most appropriate word from each one.

1 Before (school, bed, dark) each (morning, today, clock) I feed the (birds, televisions, weeds) with corn and bread.

2 In our (garden, jar, bathroom) we have a (sponge, toothbrush, pond) with lots of (sweets, frogs, books) in it.

3 He left his (flowers, bag, brother) full of (stones, books, water) on the morning (bus, cat, cake).

4 Please may (I, me, us) have a (slice, turnip, tadpole) of (moles, house, cake)?

5 Dad puts our (car, cabbage, fire) into the (tin, garage, balloon) every (button, night, moment).

6 At the end of the (road, bath, meal) we helped to (paint, break, clear) the (rose, table, clip).

6

Choose the word or phrase that makes each sentence true.

Example A LIBRARY always has (posters, a carpet, <u>books</u>, DVDs, stairs).

> Think about what the word in capitals <u>has</u> to have.

7 A TABLE always has (a lamp, a cloth, legs, breakfast, blue chairs).

8 A TREE always has (roots, apples, pears, a bird's nest, pink flowers).

9 A CAT always has (a mouse, claws, a thin tail, blue eyes, kittens).

10 A SNOWMAN always has (buttons, a garden, a carrot nose, a body, a long scarf).

11 A WORD always has (an 'x', a book, a page, paragraphs, letters).

12 A ZOO always has (ice creams, crowds, cars, kangaroos, animals).

6

12

Underline two words, one from each group, that go together to form a new word. The word in the first group always comes first.

Example (hand, <u>green</u>, for)   (light, <u>house</u>, sure)

13 (break, snap, mend)   (slow, fast, trip)

14 (play, hedge, bark)   (make, moon, hog)

15 (every, end, else)   (think, thin, thing)

16 (rose, very, car)   (rot, flower, stem)

17 (keep, him, cook)   (mat, self, table)

18 (pig, sheep, goose)   (lambs, lets, pet)

> Take one word at a time from the left brackets and put it in front of each of the words in the right brackets.

6

Underline the one word in each group that **cannot be made** from the letters of the word in capital letters.

Example STATIONERY   stone   tyres   ration   <u>nation</u>   noisy

19 SYMBOL   lob   boy   sob   may   mob

20 WAFFLE   law   few   ewe   awe   ale

21 FINGER   fin   fen   fir   fee   fig

22 POISON   nip   mop   pin   sip   son

23 GRATER   tar   rag   get   are   rot

24 WIZARD   raw   rid   dry   war   wad

> Look for any letters that are not in the word in capitals, and for repeats of letters.

6

Underline the one word in each group that **can be made** from the letters of the word in capital letters.

Example CHAMPION   camping   notch   peach   cramp   <u>chimp</u>

25 ZODIAC   zip   cab   cod   ice   ace

26 VIRTUE   try   vat   tar   rue   use

27 LIGHTS   sag   hit   sir   hat   gas

28 BARROW   won   web   war   owe   are

29 JIGGLE   egg   get   jet   ice   lug

30 STRAWS   wet   two   row   sit   ass

6

Focus test 6 Finding words

Change one word so that the sentence makes sense. Underline the word you are taking out and write your new word on the line.

Example I waited in line to buy a <u>book</u> to see the film.   <u>ticket</u>

> *Read the sentence and look for the part that doesn't make sense.*

1 My Alsatian puppy will grow up to be a big cat.   _____

2 The green balloon on our lawn has grown so long
   with all this rain!   _____

3 We collected sticks and built a small icicle at our
   campsite to keep us warm.   _____

4 We waited fifteen minutes at the bus start for the
   bus to come.   _____

5 Many trees drop their purses in winter time.   _____   **5**

Find the three-letter word that can be added to the letters in capitals to make a new word. The new word will complete the sentence sensibly.

Example The cat sprang onto the MO.   <u>USE</u>

> *Use the sense of the sentence to help you give a sensible answer.*

6 The mermaid sat on the rock and COM her golden hair. _____

7 The sun SS below the horizon.   _____

8 Would you like a piece of bread and TER?   _____

9 I like to watch TOONS on the television.   _____

10 The gardener dug the flowerbed with a large SE.   _____   **5**

Find a word that can be put in front of each of the following words to make new, compound words.

Example cast   fall   ward   pour   <u>down</u>

> *Try to make a sensible answer. Look for common words such as black/white, on/in, and so on.*

11 teacher   master   mate   room   _____

12 chair   spin   base   barrow   _____

13	stairs	hill	hearted	wind	_____
14	ache	butt	quarters	strong	_____
15	beat	break	burn	less	_____

⑤

Change the first word of the third pair in the same way as the other pairs to give a new word.

> Look at how the letters have been changed and continue the pattern. Take care with letter order.

Example bind, hind   bare, hare   but, <u>hut</u>

16	task, tank	flask, flank	bask, _____
17	ten, net	pot, top	ton, _____
18	prim, trim	pale, tale	pool, _____
19	comb, come	vast, vase	wish, _____
20	camera, era	parrot, rot	carpet, _____

⑤

Look at the first group of three words. The word in the middle has been made from the two other words. Complete the second group of three words in the same way, making a new word in the middle.

Example PAIN   INTO   T<u>OO</u>K   ALSO   <u>SOON</u>   ONLY

> Letter by letter, see where the middle word gets its letters from. Repeat the pattern for the second group of words.

21	GONE	GOAT	FLAT	LAIR	_____	PINE
22	CORK	CORN	NICE	PINK	_____	TOMB
23	BALL	BIKE	HIKE	FOOT	_____	WISH
24	GLAD	GLOW	CROW	HELM	_____	SPAR
25	RAFT	SOFT	SOME	CLIP	_____	SNOW

⑤

Change the first word into the last word, by changing one letter at a time and making a new, different word in the middle.

Example CASE   <u>CASH</u>   LASH

> Write down the letters that remain the same. Substitute the remaining letters one at a time.

26	BUSH	_____	DUST
27	NICE	_____	FINE
28	FIVE	_____	LOVE
29	MEET	_____	MEAN
30	DRIP	_____	TRAP

⑤

> In codes questions, numbers, symbols or other letters replace the letters in words.

If the code for TURNIP is 7 9 2 5 1 0, what are the codes for the following words?

   1 RUN _____   **2** PIT _____

   3 Using the same code, what does 2 1 0 stand for? _____   ◯ 3

If the code for BATTLE is * ~ > > @ <, what do the following codes stand for?

   4 * ~ > _____

   5 @ < > _____

   6 > ~ * _____

   7 Using the same code, what is the code for TEA? _____   ◯ 4

These words have been written in code, but the codes are not written under the right words. Match the right code to each word given below.

> Start by looking for letters that stand out, such as double letters and letters that are repeated.

HOOD	HANDY	SHOOK
N M L L J	M L L B	M P X B F

   8 M P X B F _____   **9** M L L B _____

  10 N M L L J _____

Using the same code, what do the following codes stand for?

  11 B P N M _____   **12** N L P J _____   ◯ 5

Complete the following sentences in the best way by choosing one word from each set of brackets.

Example   Tall is to (tree, <u>short</u>, colour) as narrow is to (thin, white, <u>wide</u>).

> Look for the relationship between the pairs of statements. The second pairing must be completed in the same way as the first.

13 Hat is to (head, needle, toe) as glove is to (eyes, garage, hand).

14 Bus is to (canal, park, road) as boat is to (sky, lake, tree).

15 Left is to (wrong, right, bike) as black is to (nought, garden, white).

16 Pen is to (write, pencil, vein) as brush is to (paint, yellow, path).

4

Find the missing letters and numbers. The alphabet has been written out to help you.

A B C D E F G H I J K L M N O P Q R S T U V W X Y Z

Example   AB is to CD as PQ is to <u>RS</u>.

17 BC is to DE as FG is to _____.

18 A4 is to B3 as C2 is to _____.

19 HG is to FE as DC is to _____.

20 AC is to EG as IK is to _____.

> Look for the pattern in these sequences. It may help to put your finger on the alphabet line and count the number of spaces.

4

Find the next two pairs of letters in the following sequences. The alphabet has been written out to help you.

A B C D E F G H I J K L M N O P Q R S T U V W X Y Z

Example	CQ	DP	EQ	FP	<u>GQ</u>	<u>HP</u>
21	AB	CD	EF	GH	____	____
22	ZY	XW	VU	TS	____	____
23	BD	FH	JL	NP	____	____
24	BM	CN	BO	CP	____	____
25	AP	BQ	CR	DS	____	____
26	ZT	YS	XR	WQ	____	____

> In these sequences, the letters in each pair are working separately.

6

Find the two missing numbers in the following sequences.

Example	2	4	6	8	<u>10</u>	<u>12</u>
27	1	3	____	7	____	11
28	8	12	16	____	24	____
29	____	50	40	____	20	10
30	____	____	15	20	25	30

> Look for the pattern between the numbers.

4

If a = 1, b = 2, c = 3 and d = 4, what are the values of these calculations?

> Replace the letters with numbers and work out the calculations.

1 b + c + d = _____

2 c × d = _____

3 (d + b) ÷ c = _____

4 (d − a) − b = _____

If G = 5, A = 2, B = 4, L = 3 and E = 1, what are the totals of these words?

> Add each of the letter values together to make a word total.

5 bag _____

6 ale _____

7 leg _____

8 egg _____

Eleanor and Ethan have blue pencil cases.
Josh and Eleanor have ten coloured pencils.
Ethan and Susie have twelve coloured pencils.
Susie and Josh have clear pencil cases.

> First, write down the children's names and list what they each have.

Which child has:

9 a blue pencil case and ten coloured pencils? _____

10 a clear pencil case and twelve coloured pencils? _____

11 a blue pencil case and twelve coloured pencils? _____

12 a clear pencil case and ten coloured pencils? _____

Will and Eva play football every day, except Sunday. Below is a chart of the goals they score in one week.

	MON	TUE	WED	THUR	FRI	SAT
WILL	0	6	7	3	2	4
EVA	5	2	4	3	6	0

13 How many more goals did Will score than Eva on Wednesday? _____

14 On which day did Eva score most goals? _____

15 How many goals were scored altogether on Tuesday? _____

16 Who scored the most goals during the week? _____

Here is a train timetable.

TURNEY (depart)	09:30	11:00	12:30	14:00
BARTON (arrive)	10:00	11:30	13:00	14:30

Count the minutes carefully and note when you start a new hour.

17 How long does the journey take from Turney to Barton? _____

18 If the 14:00 train arrived ten minutes late, what time
   would it arrive at Barton? _____

19 If I needed to be on time for an appointment in Barton at
   midday, which is the latest train I could catch from Turney? _____ (3

At an athletics meeting, there are four running tracks going anti-clockwise.
Track 1 is on the inside and track 4 is on the outside. There are four runners:
red, blue, yellow and green.

Red is next to blue. Red is nearer the inside of the track than blue.
Blue is not on the outside or inside track.
Yellow is between blue and green.
Green is not next to blue or red.

Who started on:

20 track 1? _____   21 track 2? _____

22 track 3? _____   23 track 4? _____

24 Which runner was not next to yellow? _____ (5

If yesterday was Wednesday, answer these questions.

Before you start, work out the day today and write the days in order.

25 Which day of the week will it be in a week's time? _____

26 What is the day tomorrow? _____

27 What is the day after tomorrow? _____ (3

Aiden has 10p more than Jacob, who has 20p less than Grace. Grace has
50p. How much does each person have?

Start from the definite information you know.

28 Jacob? _____   29 Aiden? _____

30 If Chloe was 2 when her brother, Ryan, was
   born and she is 4 now, how old is Ryan? _____ (3

Now go to the Progress Chart to record your score!   Total (30

Mixed paper 1

Rearrange the muddled letters in capitals to make a proper word. The answer will complete the sentence sensibly.

Example   A BEZAR is an animal with stripes.   <u>ZEBRA</u>

1   A RNTAI runs on tracks and carries people from station
to station.   _____

2   A ERULR helps you to draw straight lines.   _____

3   A library is full of KSOBO.   _____

4   A TKTIEN is a baby cat.   _____

5   My bedroom DWOWIN has yellow curtains.   _____   ⬤ 5

If these words are placed in alphabetical order, underline the word that comes second.

6   mood   herd   food   said   tend

7   sigh   here   mess   warm   jump

8   lump   bark   hole   meet   cave

9   fear   hear   dear   pear   wear

10 bung   bump   band   bell   bird   ⬤ 5

Add one letter to the word in capital letters to make a new word. The meaning of the new word is given in the clue.

Example   PLAN   simple   <u>PLAIN</u>

11 BEAD   basic food   _____

12 DUTY   powdery   _____

13 HITS   clues, tips   _____

14 DUET   bed covering   _____

15 WELL   live, reside   _____   ⬤ 5

20

Look at these groups of words.

A	B	C
Fish	Colours	Relations

Choose the correct group for each of the words below. Write in the letter.

16 brother ___   yellow ___

17 trout ___   green ___

18 grandmother ___   father ___

19 uncle ___   purple ___

20 haddock ___   niece ___

5

Look at the first group of three words. The word in the middle has been made from the two other words. Complete the second group of three words in the same way, making a new word in the middle.

Example PAIN INTO T<u>OO</u>K   ALSO <u>SOON</u> ONLY

21 WELL WEST HOST   HINT _____ MULL

22 SOAK SOAP GRIP   WANE _____ FLAT

23 BOOK TOOL TAIL   FEET _____ WASP

24 SOCK BACK BALL   NICE _____ RAIL

25 SACK BACK BITE   FARM _____ HUSH

5

Emily and Abdul have green sweatshirts.

Thea and Emily have leggings.

Abdul and Jacob have jeans.

Jacob and Thea have blue sweatshirts.

Which child has:

26 a green sweatshirt and leggings? _____

27 a blue sweatshirt and jeans? _____

28 a green sweatshirt and jeans? _____

29 a blue sweatshirt and leggings? _____

4

Choose the word or phrase that makes each sentence true.

Example A LIBRARY always has (posters, a carpet, <u>books</u>, DVDs, stairs).

30 A NEWSPAPER always has (pictures, puzzles, a television guide, articles, a business section).

31 A DUCKLING always has (a pond, brothers, grey feathers, bread, a beak).

32 A MOUNTAIN always has (snow, a summit, hikers, footpaths, cable cars).

33 A COUNTRY always has (tigers, a flag, a sea border, a queen, a foreign language).

34 An AEROPLANE always has (wings, passengers, missiles, films, duty-free goods).

35 A KNIFE always has a (fork, a chopping board, a blade, a sheath, a black handle).

(6)

If the code for CARTON is 4 6 2 9 1 8, what are the codes for the following words?

36 NOT _____

37 RAN _____

38 COT _____

39 CAR _____

40 ART _____

(5)

Underline the two words, one from each group, that are the most similar in meaning.

Example (race, shop, <u>start</u>)   (finish, <u>begin</u>, end)

41 (wind, blow, sugar)   (blue, puff, salt)

42 (pinch, steal, take)   (give, soft, nip)

43 (borrow, lend, left)   (loan, right, live)

44 (with, want, warn)   (design, desire, dislike)

45 (saw, sore, say)   (painful, clear, blame)

(5)

Mixed paper 2

If K = 2, L = 4, M = 1 and N = 3, what are the values of these calculations?

1 L + K + M = ____

2 N × L = ____

3 (N + M) ÷ K = ____

4 (N − K) + L = ____

5 (K × L) − (M × N) = ____

⑤

Which one letter can be added to the front of all of these words to make new words?

Example	_C_are	_C_at	_C_rate	_C_all	_C_
6	__ark	__right	__lazing	__and	____
7	__core	__lightly	__lumber	__ailed	____
8	__angle	__each	__rail	__axed	____
9	__ode	__udder	__oar	__ink	____
10	__ours	__ears	__earn	__awning	____

⑤

Underline two words, one from each group, that go together to form a new word. The word in the first group always comes first.

Example (hand, <u>green</u>, for)   (light, <u>house</u>, sure)

11 (rough, micro, side)   (sea, wave, sand)

12 (pine, ripe, ant)   (pear, plum, apple)

13 (not, nit, net)   (fish, eye, ball)

③

Fill in the crosswords so that all the given words are included. You have been given one letter as a clue in each crossword.

14 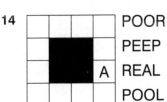 POOR
PEEP
REAL
POOL

15 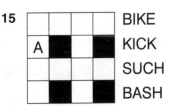 BIKE
KICK
SUCH
BASH

②

23

Underline the two words, one from each group, that are the most opposite in meaning.

Example (dawn, <u>early</u>, wake)   (<u>late</u>, stop, sunrise)

16 (empty, spiky, tidy)   (neat, messy, hollow)

17 (unattractive, clean, broad)   (dirty, bright, calm)

18 (polished, yellow, plastic)   (reflective, dull, shiny)

19 (unwell, after, midday)   (sickly, noon, before)

20 (sweet, acidic, brainy)   (clever, tight, sour)   **5**

If the code for LABELS is $\Delta\ \alpha\ \Omega\ \theta\ \Delta\ \Pi$, what do the following codes stand for?

21 $\Pi\ \theta\ \alpha$ _____

22 $\theta\ \theta\ \Delta$ _____

23 $\alpha\ \Pi\ \Pi$ _____

24 $\Omega\ \alpha\ \Delta\ \Delta$ _____

25 $\Pi\ \alpha\ \Delta\ \theta$ _____   **5**

Find the three-letter word that can be added to the letters in capitals to make a new word. The new word will complete the sentence sensibly.

Example The cat sprang onto the MO.   <u>USE</u>

26 In the FYARD was a brand new blue tractor.   _____

27 The human skeleton has 206 BS.   _____

28 A plank on the FOOTBGE was rotten and unsafe.   _____

29 Can you PICT this week's lottery numbers?   _____

30 We run around in the PGROUND at break time.   _____   **5**

In each line, underline the word that has its letters in alphabetical order.

31 were   fist   your   waxy

32 zips   wash   draw   most

33 toil   farm   film   yell

34 hard   moth   cosy   page

35 buoy   band   bike   best   **5**

Underline the two words that are the odd ones out in the following group of words.

Example black   <u>king</u>   purple   green   <u>house</u>

36	blue	sky	cloud	green	yellow
37	knife	fork	pencil	cloth	spoon
38	moth	glide	fly	bee	brush
39	train	bus	car	road	tracks
40	squeeze	squash	lemonade	bottle	milk

5

Complete the following sentences by selecting the most sensible word from each group of words given in the brackets. Underline the words selected.

Example The (<u>children</u>, boxes, foxes) carried the (houses, <u>books</u>, steps) home from the (greengrocer, <u>library</u>, factory).

41 The (woman, man, dog) read his (magazine, lake, car) on the (house, car, bus).

42 The grey (mice, jeans, clouds) gathered overhead and suddenly it began to (rain, climb, cry) very (slowly, cleverly, heavily).

43 She left her (elephant, wardrobe, cardigan) in our (fridge, picture frame, car) after (tomorrow, ballet, noon).

44 At the end of the (day, month, year) the (stars, sun, moon) sets over the (dog, horizon, mat).

45 We (crossed, jumped, crawled) the (hall, road, church) on the (antelope, zebra, buffalo) crossing.

5

Mixed paper 3

A B C D E F G H I J K L M N O P Q R S T U V W X Y Z

Imagine the last three letters of the alphabet are removed. Answer these questions.

1 Which would be the second to last letter of those left? Circle the correct letter.

    V   U   W   X

2 Which is the one after the middle letter in the new alphabet? Circle the correct letter.

    K   L   M   N

    2

Fill in the crosswords so that all the given words are included. You have been given one letter as a clue in each crossword.

3    DUST   **4** 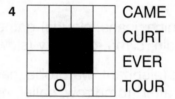   CAME

PUMA   CURT

STAY   EVER

MANY   TOUR

5    BUSY

BARN

SORT

RARE

    3

Find the three-letter word that can be added to the letters in capitals to make a new word. The new word will complete the sentence sensibly.

Example   The cat sprang onto the MO.   <u>USE</u>

6 The firefighter was very brave and COUROUS.   _____

7 Please may I borrow your pencil SHARER?   _____

8 Can you tell me WE the nearest post office is?   _____

9 The PAVET outside school is uneven in places.   _____

10 The sun is setting and it is getting DER.   _____

    5

Find the letter that will end the first word and start the second word.

Example drow (<u>n</u>) ought

11 crim (___) arly

12 flowe (___) iver

13 peac (___) oney

14 shrim (___) art

15 pani (___) ream

5

Underline the two words in each sentence that need to change places for the sentence to make sense.

Example She went to <u>letter</u> the <u>write</u>.

16 He put on his laces and tied his shoe.

17 He twisted and fell his ankle.

18 We leave to need at half past nine.

19 She had a mosquito large bite on her arm.

20 They wandered across the rug and laid out the picnic grass.

5

Here is a train timetable.

BOLLOW (depart)	STANTWAY (arrive)
09:10	10:00
09:40	10:30
10:10	11:00
10:40	11:30
11:10	12:00

21 How long does the journey take from Bollow to Stantway?   _____

22 If the 10:10 train arrived ten minutes late, what time would it arrive at Stantway?   _____

23 If I needed to be on time for an appointment in Stantway at 10.45, which is the latest train I could catch from Bollow?   _____

24 The trains leave Bollow every _____ minutes.

25 If the timetable followed the same pattern, when would the next train arrive at Stantway after the midday one?   _____

5

Underline the pair of words that are the most similar in meaning.

Example come, go   <u>roams, wanders</u>   fear, fare

26	bent, twisted	ascend, descend	go, stop
27	question, answer	morning, afternoon	idle, lazy
28	beautiful, attractive	king, queen	poor, rich
29	mouldy, fresh	serious, sincere	active, still
30	old, young	rainy, cloudy	bold, brave

⬤ 5

These words have been written in code, but the codes are not written under the right words. Match the right code to each word given below.

FLUFF	FAIR	RAIL	FULL	LAIR
S O Z K	K O Z B	B O Z K	S B T S S	S T B B

31 S O Z K _____   32 K O Z B _____

33 B O Z K _____   34 S B T S S _____

35 S T B B _____

⬤ 5

Underline the pair of words that are the most opposite in meaning.

Example cup, mug   coffee, milk   <u>hot, cold</u>

36	work, rest	ribbon, string	tear, rip
37	swift, rapid	top, bottom	plate, dish
38	bind, tie	grow, increase	catch, throw
39	cute, pretty	ugly, beautiful	handsome, good looking
40	wan, pale	wash, clean	heavy, light

⬤ 5

Underline the one word in each group that **cannot be made** from the letters of the word in capital letters.

Example STATIONERY   stone   tyres   ration   <u>nation</u>   noisy

41	MOTHER	her	the	rot	rat	ore
42	PIECES	pie	see	sip	sap	ice
43	PLUMES	sum	sue	mop	emu	sup
44	FLARES	see	ear	elf	are	far
45	WOBBLE	ebb	owl	bow	woe	bed

⬤ 5

Mixed paper 4

Change one word so that the sentence makes sense. Underline the word you are taking out and write your new word on the line.

Example I waited in line to buy a <u>book</u> to see the film.   *ticket*

1 We were caught in the rainstorm and got soaking dry.   _____

2 Squares have four sides and three right angles.   _____

3 The mother duck took her tiny, fluffy calves for a swim on the pond.   _____

4 The cyclist wore a safety helmet on his foot.   _____

5 When traffic lights turn from green to red, it means you must go.   _____   5

A B C D E F G H I J K L M N O P Q R S T U V W X Y Z

Answer these alphabet questions.

6 Which month of the year begins with the sixth letter?   _____

7 Which season of the year begins with the twenty-third letter?   _____

8 Which day of the week has seven letters?   _____

9 If the days of the week are put in alphabetical order, which comes second?   _____

10 If the seasons are put in alphabetical order, which comes second?   _____   5

Rearrange the muddled words in capital letters so that each sentence makes sense.

Example There are sixty SNODCES <u>seconds</u> in a UTMINE <u>minute</u>.

11 We love to kick the leaves that have FLENAL _____ from the

RETSE _____ in the park.

12 It is already FLAH _____ past VNESE _____ in the evening.

13 My bicycle HLEEW _____ is bent so I am BALUEN _____ to ride it to school.

29

14 The CHLUN _____ Dad is cooking SLEMLS _____ delicious.

15 In the GRIPNS _____, baby DRIBS _____ hatch.

5

Complete the following sentences by selecting the most sensible word from each group of words given in the brackets. Underline the words selected.

Example The (<u>children</u>, boxes, foxes) carried the (houses, <u>books</u>, steps) home from the (greengrocer, <u>library</u>, factory).

16 Please (stand, sit, jump) down on that comfy (stone, table, chair) and tell me all (through, from, about) it.

17 My little (cat, giraffe, flower) eats a lot of (grass, food, sand) for a small (plant, animal, person).

18 The white (ghosts, pictures, lines) on the (car, road, legs) show drivers where to (jump, go, fly).

19 We went to the (cinema, market, post office) and bought some (cars, stamps, fruit) to post a (steering wheel, lemon, parcel).

20 We (watched, ate, ran) a firework (bin, mouse, display) in our local (station, park, hall).

5

Add one letter to the word in capital letters to make a new word. The meaning of the new word is given in the clue.

Example PLAN   simple   <u>PLAIN</u>

21 AIRY   covered with hair   _____

22 SILL   tip over   _____

23 CURE   swear   _____

24 REED   intense desire for food   _____

25 PEAL   foot-operated lever for a bike   _____

5

If a = 1, e = 2, t = 3, r = 4 and s = 5, what are the totals of these words?

26 are   ____

27 set   ____

28 rat   ____

29 tear   ____

30 star   ____

5

Underline the pair of words that are the most similar in meaning.

Example   come, go   roams, wanders   fear, fare

31 whisper, argue   guess, gloss   call, shout

32 bring, crowd   simple, hard   describe, explain

33 tearful, happy   similar, alike   reason, ask

34 slip, slide   buy, by   quick, quite

35 brown, yellow   hit, strike   grass, tree

5

Find the next two pairs of letters in the following sequences. The alphabet has been written out to help you.

A B C D E F G H I J K L M N O P Q R S T U V W X Y Z

Example   CQ   DP   EQ   FP   GQ   HP

36 GO   RP   GQ   RR   ____   ____

37 MM   NN   OO   PP   ____   ____

38 DF   HJ   LN   PR   ____   ____

39 AZ   BY   CX   DW   ____   ____

40 FQ   GW   HQ   IW   ____   ____

5

Underline the one word in the brackets that is the most opposite in meaning to the word in capitals.

Example   WIDE   (broad   vague   long   narrow   motorway)

41 WEAK   (feeble   little   quiet   loud   powerful)

42 BREAK   (pause   try   mend   see   beat)

43 TRUTHFUL   (distant   disappear   describe   dishonest   discard)

44 SILENCE   (peace   quiet   noise   thunder   note)

45 SOLID   (hard   firm   rigid   liquid   icy)

5

Mixed paper 5

Class 1 and Class 2 chose their favourite days at school. Below is a chart of the results.

	MON	TUE	WED	THUR	FRI
CLASS 1	0	6	7	9	8
CLASS 2	4	3	5	8	10

1 How many more prefer Wednesday in Class 1 than in Class 2? _____

2 Which day does Class 1 like best? _____

3 How many children altogether chose Friday? _____

4 How many children are there in each class? _____

5 After Monday, which was the next least-popular day? _____   5

Underline the two words, one from each group, that are the most similar in meaning.

Example   (race, shop, <u>start</u>)   (finish, <u>begin</u>, end)

6 (space, quick, stuffed)   (eager, gap, mobile)

7 (bitter, bright, strong)   (weak, sturdy, feeble)

8 (spare, endless, ever)   (wide, crude, extra)

9 (gain, grind, spin)   (top, revolve, corner)

10 (gather, hide, scatter)   (spread, mince, cook)   5

Find the missing letters. The alphabet has been written out to help you.

A B C D E F G H I J K L M N O P Q R S T U V W X Y Z

Example   AB is to CD as PQ is to <u>RS</u>.

11 MN is to OP as VW is to ___.

12 KM is to OQ as SU is to ___.

13 NM is to LK as GF is to ___.

14 MO is to QS as BD is to ___.

15 VW is to XY as JK is to ___.   5

Underline the two words in each line that are made from the same letters.

Example TAP   PET   <u>TEA</u>   POT   <u>EAT</u>

16 SKID   SHED   DESK   DASH   DISK

17 MOOD   MEAD   DOOM   DEEM   MEET

18 BORE   ROTE   ROPE   TORE   SORE

19 PEST   PORT   STEP   PAST   TRAP

20 PORE   FOAM   FROM   POEM   MOPE   ◯ 5

If the code for SALMON is 4 6 8 3 5 1, what are the codes for the following words?

21 MAN _____   22 LOAN _____

Using the same code, what do the following codes stand for?

23 4 5 1 _____   24 4 8 6 3 _____   25 6 8 4 5 _____   ◯ 5

Remove one letter from the word in capital letters to leave a new word. The meaning of the new word is given in the clue.

Example AUNT   an insect   <u>ANT</u>

26 CHEAP   a pile   _____

27 LAPSE   more than one circuit of a track   _____

28 GRAVE   handed over   _____

29 STRAY   remain   _____

30 LEAST   final   _____   ◯ 5

Look at the first group of three words. The word in the middle has been made from the two other words. Complete the second group of three words in the same way, making a new word in the middle.

Example PA<u>IN</u>   INTO   <u>TO</u>OK   ALSO   <u>SOON</u>   ONLY

31 JUMP   JUST   STEW   MEND   _____   ETCH

32 BOIL   RIOT   RUST   BORN   _____   FILM

33 KISS   BOSS   BOND   FIZZ   _____   JAMS

34 TINY   FACT   FACE   KING   _____   MILE

35 COSY   MOST   TRIM   WANE   _____   KERB   ◯ 5

33

If the letters in the following words are arranged in alphabetical order, which letter comes second?

36 ACTOR ____

37 BISON ____

38 DWARF ____

39 UNCLE ____

40 PROUD ____

( ) 5

Change the first word of the third pair in the same way as the other pairs to give a new word.

Example bind, hind   bare, hare   but, _hut_

41 cat, pat   cut, put   cot, _____

42 fight, flight fat, flat   few, _____

43 ram, rum   task, tusk   bat, _____

44 unto, to   spin, in   pram, _____

45 anger, manger any, many   an, _____

( ) 5

Mixed paper 6

Change the first word into the last word, by changing one letter at a time and making a new, different word in the middle.

Example CASE　　　　<u>CASH</u>　　　LASH

1 PILL　　　―――――　　　FILM

2 COME　　　―――――　　　CORN

3 HUSH　　　―――――　　　POSH

4 FURY　　　―――――　　　BURN

5 CAKE　　　―――――　　　PAGE

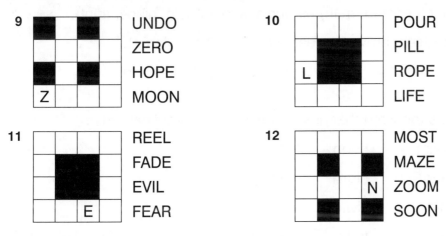

5

Underline the word in each line that uses only the first six letters of the alphabet.

6 pot　　　gym　　　sad　　　fed

7 dry　　　ace　　　box　　　ham

8 fun　　　elf　　　ass　　　bee

3

Fill in the crosswords so that all the given words are included. You have been given one or two letters as a clue in each crossword.

9

		UNDO
Z		ZERO
		HOPE
		MOON

10

		POUR
L		PILL
		ROPE
		LIFE

11

		REEL
		FADE
		EVIL
E		FEAR

12

		MOST
		MAZE
N		ZOOM
		SOON

4

35

If yesterday was Friday, answer these questions.

13 Which day of the week will it be in a week's time? _____

14 What is the day tomorrow? _____

15 What is the day after tomorrow? _____ ◯ 3

Underline the pair of words that are the most opposite in meaning.

Example cup, mug   coffee, milk   <u>hot, cold</u>

16 straight, curved   tea, coffee   came, come

17 distant, far   ceiling, floor   care, love

18 gold, silver   life, death   here, hear

19 hill, valley   smile, laugh   arm, tepid

20 off, of   kind, sort   agree, differ ◯ 5

Complete the following sentences in the best way by choosing one word from each set of brackets.

Example Tall is to (tree, <u>short</u>, colour) as narrow is to (thin, white, <u>wide</u>).

21 Cut is to (hair, knife, knee) as scoop is to (spoon, swoon, saloon).

22 Book is to (word, read, story) as television is to (sit, colour, watch).

23 Father is to (mother, dad, man) as uncle is to (cousin, niece, aunt).

24 Eye is to (blink, see, brown) as ear is to (hear, head, large).

25 Scale is to (kitchen, fish, hill) as feather is to (quill, bird, fur). ◯ 5

In each line, underline the word that has its letters in alphabetical order.

26 idea   calm   hung   flux

27 gone   flop   high   soup

28 kilt   dirt   kiwi   wise

29 path   thin   fort   edge

30 book   hilt   grab   cane ◯ 5

Find the letter that will end the first word and start the second word.

Example drow (<u>n</u>) ought

31 flavou (__) ose

32 burs (__) ame

33 us (__) verywhere

34 bi (__) iraffe

35 sno (__) aterfall

Underline two words, one from each group, that go together to form a new word. The word in the first group always comes first.

Example (hand, <u>green</u>, for)   (light, <u>house</u>, sure)

36 (note, post, card)   (bend, lit, board)

37 (fire, fierce, find)   (fighter, friend, fixer)

38 (over, by, with)   (hear, here, there)

39 (fore, four, for)   (three, always, ever)

40 (be, by, above)   (come, go, leave)

If $f = 5$, $g = 4$, $h = 2$ and $e = 3$, what are the values of these calculations?

41 $f + g + e =$ _____

42 $g \times e =$ _____

43 $(h + g) \div e =$ _____

44 $(f - h) + g =$ _____

45 $(g \times f) - (h \times e) =$ _____

Mixed paper 7

Underline the two words in each line that are made from the same letters.

Example TAP   PET   <u>TEA</u>   POT   <u>EAT</u>

1	HOLD	DRAG	GOLD	CASK	SACK
2	SOLE	TOOL	SLOT	LOSE	SELL
3	GLOW	WOLF	FOOL	TONG	FLOW
4	OWLS	HOWL	SLOW	SHOW	MOTH
5	LORE	RULE	LURE	PURE	ROPE

○ 5

Cameron has 30p more than Amber, who has 60p less than Taj. Taj has £1.50.

6 How much does Amber have? _____

7 How much does Cameron have? _____

Farmer X sells twenty more sheep at the market than Farmer Y, who sells ten fewer than Farmer Z. Farmer Z sells fifty sheep at the market.

8 How many sheep does Farmer Y sell? _____

9 How many sheep does Farmer X sell? _____

10 If Sinead was 12 when her brother, Alex, was born and she is 15 now, how old is Alex? _____

○ 5

Underline the one word in each group that **can be made** from the letters of the word in capital letters.

Example CHAMPION   camping   notch   peach   cramp   <u>chimp</u>

11	GROWLS	low	for	gel	ore	leg
12	MARKET	kit	ram	try	ask	tie
13	DROOPY	you	ode	rap	pry	rid
14	CLAMPS	mop	sat	sum	spy	cap
15	BRIDGE	gem	dim	bet	big	ego

○ 5

38

Change the first word of the third pair in the same way as the other pairs to give a new word.

Example bind, hind   bare, hare   but, <u>hut</u>

16 feast, east   flight, light   fall, _____

17 tap, pat   war, raw   but, _____

18 when, then   west, test   will, _____

19 end, bend   oat, boat   lack, _____

20 often, ten   grate, ate   stone, _____

5

Underline the pair of words that are the most opposite in meaning.

Example cup, mug   coffee, milk   <u>hot, cold</u>

21 bumpy, smooth   difficult, tricky   easy, simple

22 key, quay   long, short   stopped, finished

23 staying, remaining   flying, gliding   laughing, crying

24 besides, upon   beyond, above   far, near

25 bite, chew   head, face   on, off

5

These words have been written in code, but the codes are not written under the right words. Match the right code to each word given below.

BRAIN	CRAB	RAIN	BARN	RAINY
9 3 6 2	5 9 3 6 2	9 3 6 2 1	8 9 3 5	5 3 9 2

26 9 3 6 2   _____

27 5 9 3 6 2   _____

28 9 3 6 2 1   _____

29 8 9 3 5   _____

30 5 3 9 2   _____

5

Find the two missing numbers in the following sequences.

Example 2   4   6   8   <u>10</u>   <u>12</u>

31 11   22   33   44   ___   ___

32 27   29   ___   33   ___   37

33 ___   15   ___   11   9   7

34 ___   ___   24   28   32   36

35 16   ___   36   46   ___   66

○ 5

Remove one letter from the word in capital letters to leave a new word. The meaning of the new word is given in the clue.

Example AUNT   an insect   <u>ANT</u>

36 WITCH   accompanied by   _____

37 BLINK   join up   _____

38 CLAMP   applaud   _____

39 DROOP   fall   _____

40 HEDGE   outside rim   _____

○ 5

Underline the word in each line that uses three vowels.

41 worthy   harden   wreath   violet

42 stupid   cranes   police   brains

43 proper   plaque   craves   bleeds

44 pillow   ragged   varied   flurry

45 gained   stable   boosts   father

○ 5

Mixed paper 8

Underline the one word in each group that **can be made** from the letters of the word in capital letters.

Example	CHAMPION	camping	notch	peach	cramp	<u>chimp</u>
1	SLIGHT	leg	tag	hot	lit	ill
2	EXCEPT	cox	tap	axe	see	pet
3	JAGGED	age	dew	jar	god	dug
4	BLIGHT	get	beg	hit	bug	hug
5	LARYNX	any	nor	run	fly	tax

5

Rearrange the muddled letters in capitals to make a proper word. The answer will complete the sentence sensibly.

Example   A BEZAR is an animal with stripes.   <u>ZEBRA</u>

6 A, E, I, O, U are the five WVESLO in the alphabet.   _____

7 SDKCU are types of water birds with webbed feet.   _____

8 The moon and SSRAT are shining brightly.   _____

9 A STFAE is a large celebratory meal.   _____

10 A TCHAM is a contest in which teams compete against each other.   _____

5

Find a word that can be put in front of each of the following words to make new, compound words.

Example	cast	fall	ward	pour	<u>down</u>
11	print	tip	nail	less	_____
12	sty	tail	swill	skin	_____
13	ball	storm	drift	flake	_____
14	wood	guard	proof	work	_____
15	line	craft	port	mail	_____

5

A B C D E F G H I J K L M N O P Q R S T U V W X Y Z

Imagine the first three letters of the alphabet are removed. Answer these questions.

16 Which would be the second letter of those left? Circle the correct letter.

E   D   H   F

17 How many letters would there be in this alphabet? Circle the correct number.

22   23   24   26

2

Fill in the crosswords so that all the given words are included. You have been given one letter as a clue in each crossword.

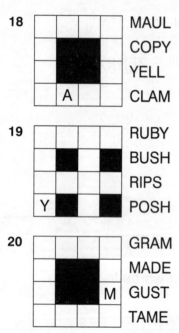

18 MAUL
COPY
YELL
CLAM

19 RUBY
BUSH
RIPS
POSH

20 GRAM
MADE
GUST
TAME

3

In a changing room there are ten pegs in two rows.
Numbers 1 to 5 are along one wall and numbers 6 to 10 are opposite.
Number 1 is opposite 6, 2 is opposite 7, and so on.
If I hang my things on peg 3 and my friend, Chiara, hangs her things on peg 4, answer the questions below.

21 What is the peg number opposite to mine? _____

22 What is the peg number opposite Chiara's? _____

If Sasha hangs her things on peg 6 and Bella hangs her things next to Chiara's, answer these questions.

23 What is Bella's peg number? _____

24 What is the peg number opposite to Bella? _____

25 Which peg is opposite Sasha's? _____

⬭ 5

Underline the one word in the brackets that is the most opposite in meaning to the word in capitals.

Example WIDE   (broad   vague   long   <u>narrow</u>   motorway)

26 EARLY   (quick   late   hurried   delay   slight)

27 UP   (high   lift   climb   beside   down)

28 STRIPED   (shy   plain   coloured   patterned   funny)

29 FULL   (brimming   replete   complete   empty   pouring)

30 PEACE   (quiet   slice   war   chunk   clapping)

⬭ 5

If the letters in the following words are arranged in alphabetical order, which letter comes third?

31 FILTH   ___

32 POEMS   ___

33 MOUTH   ___

34 CANDY   ___

35 COBRA   ___

⬭ 5

If the code for TABLES is ← → ↓ ↖ ↑ ↗, what do the following codes stand for?

36 ↗ ↑ ←   _____

37 ← ↑ →   _____

38 ↓ → ←   _____

39 → ← ↑   _____

40 ↖ ↑ ←   _____

⬭ 5

Find the next two pairs of letters in the following sequences. The alphabet has been written out to help you.

A B C D E F G H I J K L M N O P Q R S T U V W X Y Z

Example CQ   DP   EQ   FP   <u>GQ</u>   <u>HP</u>

41 BD   FH   JL   NP   ___   ___

42 SR   QP   ON   ML   ___   ___

43 AP   BQ   AR   BS   ___   ___

44 TE   RE   PE   NE   ___   ___

45 QJ   RK   SL   TM   ___   ___   ⬤ 5

Now go to the Progress Chart to record your score!   Total ⬤ 45